Purposeful Design

UNDERSTANDING *the* CREATION

Purposeful Design

UNDERSTANDING *the* CREATION

Jay Schabacker

DEDICATION

If you have wept for a loved one; if you are a son or a daughter; a son-in-law or a daughter-in-law; a grandson or a granddaughter, this book is dedicated to you. My greatest desire and wish is that each of you—in seeing the hand of our Creator— come to fully understand His finished work through His Son, our Lord and Savior, Jesus Christ.

ISBN 987-0-9896190-0-4

Jayschabacker.com

jayschab@aol.com

Book design by Kathryn E. Campbell

Printed in the United States of America

All scripture references are from the New International Version (NIV) Study Bible

CONTENTS

PREFACE

You are viewing this book because I have a passion for others—how they are doing—and how they are thinking. And, I wish everyone would have an immensely positive view of themselves, of this world that we are in, and of others—mostly because of the understanding of our own astounding and loving creation.

However, it has often concerned me that newspapers continually remind us of the negative. For example: In 2009, the city of Palo Alto, California, struggled with a rash of teen suicides. One newspaper reported, "Another Palo Alto teen has died after stepping in front of a commuter train, the fourth such suicide in less than six months."

Could it be that too many of us lack a healthy belief system that points us clearly to the good and the positive? Could it be that many of us haven't stopped to ponder what I consider to be the larger issue—the reason to live the life that God, our loving Creator and Purposeful Designer intended for us?

This book is the culmination of many happy (and challenging) hours of questioning, probing, study, research, and writing. In my mind, I started out by calling it "In the Beginning", as I wanted to bring out the fascination of the incredible six days of creation. But, when I researched the awesome book written by Walt Brown, Ph.D., titled "In the Beginning—Compelling Evidence for Creation and the Flood,"—I realized it was time to change the title of my quest to—"Understanding the Creation". Following this were the writing of a lengthy manuscript, a power point series, a web site—understandingthecreation.com, an educational video aimed at home school children,—and now this—yet another book! Another "Coffee Table" book!—"Purposeful Design".

As this project moved along, many people contributed and offered constructive assistance. First, I must acknowledge the superb research work and publications from outstanding scientists and theologians who—out of necessity—have come before me and contributed to the wealth of information that I have summarized into my works. As I hope you will peruse these other resources on your own, I have added a listing of these sources in the Bibliography towards the end of this book.

Then, no writer is an island to himself. They need literary help! And this help I received from two excellent editor/collaborators: Julie O. Link,—"editing, proofing, writing", writelinkediting.com; and Nancy Arant Williams, "freelance editor and author" (nancyarantwilliams. com). In addition, I am indebted to the expert work of Liina Koivula, Kathleen Shaputis, and Kathy Campbell of Gorham Printing (gorhamprinting.com), and also the artistic talent of my good friend, Diane Johnson, (ldianejohnson.com). Further, I am thankful for the help and encouragement given me by Bret and Jacqueline Smith of The Digital Tutor (thedigitaltutor.com).

In closing, certainly, many others have given me advice and assistance—too many to name here. But, most importantly, I am thankful for the loving, helpful and patient assistance from my wife,—Nancy Schabacker.

I am hoping you will gain encouragement from this work.

—JAY SCHABACKER
Lexington, South Carolina

The "Man in the Moon"

Have you ever wondered about the things around you? The sun, moon, and stars? About the miracle of yourself? The cause of all this—?

An Intelligent Designer? A Purposeful Designer? An all powerful God who is our creator?

To start with, how about the circuit of our moon above us—giving us light at night—and showing us its same face every time we look at it? Moons that circle around a planet appear to not rotate on their axis.

Why?

Could it be that Someone in Charge—a Purposeful Designer—wanted it that way so we his people would have a nice view—and something to marvel about?

We see the same side of the moon every time we look at it—for the same reason that we would see the same side of a railroad engine on a circular railroad track orbiting around us. The moon, like the railroad engine just keeps moving straight ahead—showing us just one side or its face—some call it the *"Man in the Moon"*.

The Moon's Orbit ➤

- The moon doesn't rotate on its axis

- It travels straight ahead in its orbit around the earth

- Like a railroad car on a circular track in its orbit around the earth, we always see the same side.

Incredible—designed with a purpose—accomplished by our Purposeful Designer just for us—you and me.

Let's now turn the pages, and review some of the Purposeful Design in the format of God's creation, and start to realize how very special that is to you and me.

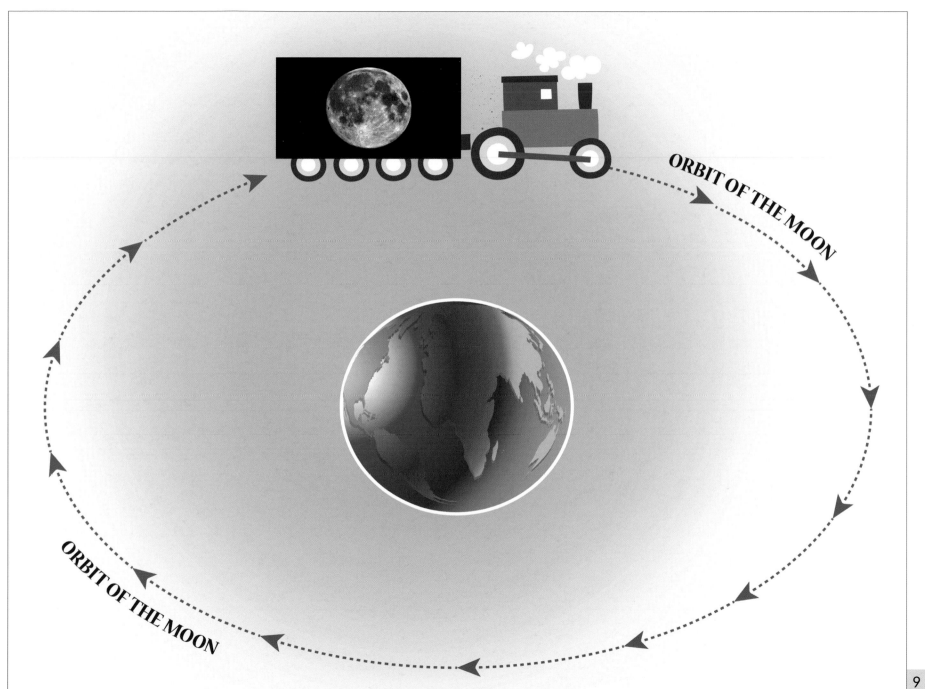

In the beginning God created the heavens and the earth.
Now the earth was formless and empty, darkness was over the surface
of the deep, and the Spirit of god was hovering over the waters.

And God said, "Let there be light," and there was light. God saw
that the light was good, and he separated the light from the darkness.
God called the light "day," and the darkness he called "night."
And there was evening, and there was morning—the first day.

GENESIS 1:1-5

CHAPTER 1

The First Day
Creation of the Heavens and the Earth
the Foundation of it All

Our Creator, God, was 100% involved in this developing creation. So much so that the writer of Genesis uses the word "hovering" to describe God's involvement. "Hovering" in the Hebrew language brings to mind an image of a hen brooding over her chicks—as God did.

All powerful God was in the process of transforming the earth from a formless and empty blob in space— to something better, more complete. And the void of darkness was filled with light, God's light, which was spoken into existence.

And although Genesis gives us a detailed account of the beginning of virtually everything, it does not discuss the origins of God, because He is eternal with no beginning and no end. Such a concept is difficult for our finite minds to grasp, but that truth is the basis upon which all other revelations are built. Rather, the passage simply explains what He did: "In the beginning God created."

What Keeps Things Going?

To put it simply, something started our solar system and something keeps it going. The second law of thermodynamics says that the energy for useful work is (and always has been) decreasing with time. If you start a top spinning it will slow down and stop.

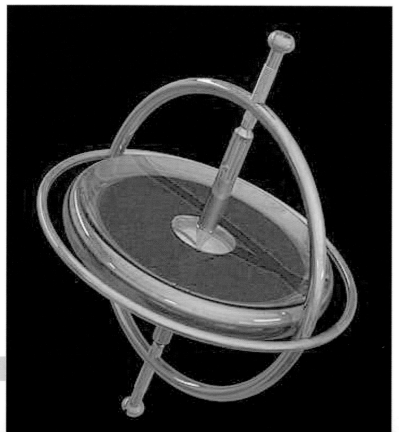

What keeps the earth, the planets, and the moon continually progressing year after year at the same constant speed and velocity?

Not a day goes by that scientists are not discovering something new about our universe. We are continually learning about new stars that we never knew existed. We are surprised to discover new plant and animal species. Such discoveries confirm that we have much more to learn about our universe than we originally thought. This only gives more credence to the notion that someone greater than mere humans planned it all—and brought it about.

Albert Einstein, a believer in intelligent design and an intelligent designer himself, once put it this way: *"The most incomprehensible thing about the universe is that it is comprehensible."*

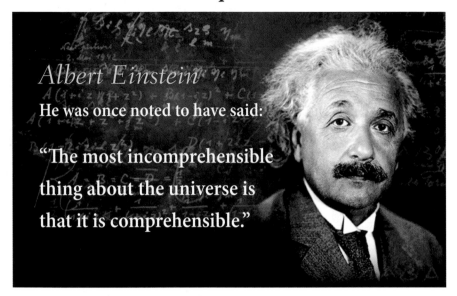

We are not in chaos. Some, Albert Einstein included, have correctly noted that our universe is orderly—and follows "rules" of nature that do not change. And, if these rules of nature did change, from time to time—in a chaotic fashion—we would really be in bad shape! And, the fact that there are rules at all is a kind of miracle.

Hence, once again, we should be thankful to a benevolent Intelligent and Purposeful Designer—God.

The earth orbits the sun at a never changing speed of 66,700 miles per hour, which is 18.5 miles per second. This orbit takes 365 days, 5 hours, 48 minutes and 46 seconds each "year," and traverses 584.3 million miles.

The earth makes one complete rotation on its axis in 23 hours, 56 minutes and 4 seconds, which is one "day." At the equator, the orbital speed of spin is 1,037.5646 miles per hour.

Our moon revolves around our earth in 27.3217 days with an orbital velocity of 2,288.16 miles per hour.

But God made the earth by his power;
he founded the world by his wisdom and
stretched out the heavens by his understanding.

JEREMIAH 10:12

15

And God said, "Let there be an expanse between the waters to separate water from water." So God made the expanse and separated the water under the expanse from the water above it. And it was so. God called the expanse "sky." And there was evening, and there was morning—the second day.

GENESIS 1:6-8

CHAPTER 2

The Second Day
Creation of the Atmosphere and Water

The second day of creation dealt with the sky and the water. It was not yet time for the creation of living things. But the preconditions for life as we know it were under way. Note that it wasn't until later—on day three, that God defined the location and limits of the water—the oceans—and the continents of dry land.

The water below sky-level was liquid (H_2O) and the water above was gaseous—water vapor, created to the extent and the exact proportions that only our Purposeful Designer could orchestrate.

With God's infinite power He needed only to speak events and actions into existence. When God speaks it is done instantly!

Quenching the Thirsty Earth—The "Rain Cycle"

The rain cycle, which is needed to sustain life, is really quite complex and could not have happened by accident. The cycle requires many ingredients: the vast oceans (71% of the earth's surface is covered by water), the sun, the earth's rotation, the wind and clouds, meteoric dust particles in the atmosphere, a warm earth and rising air currents, gravity and the dual mechanisms of evaporation and the condensation of water (H_2O).

Condensation

Precipitation

Transpiration
(evaporation from plants)

Snow and ice

Evaporation

Runoff

Infiltration
(water entering soil)

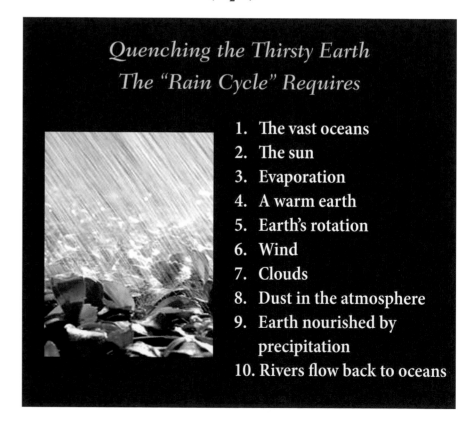

Quenching the Thirsty Earth
The "Rain Cycle" Requires

1. The vast oceans
2. The sun
3. Evaporation
4. A warm earth
5. Earth's rotation
6. Wind
7. Clouds
8. Dust in the atmosphere
9. Earth nourished by precipitation
10. Rivers flow back to oceans

Before it rains, dust particles mainly from foreign meteorite matter, attach themselves to small water particles and rising air keeps them aloft, allowing the minute particles to grow in size and gain weight. When heavy enough for gravity to overcome the upward force of rising air currents, the heavy water particles (about one tenth of an inch in diameter) fall to earth as rain.

The earth and farmland is nourished by the precipitation.

Some runoff from rain fills the streams and rivers that eventually flow back to the oceans where the water cycle is ready to begin again.

First the hot sun beats down on the oceans raising the water temperature and through evaporation—water turns to gaseous vapor—and begins to rise. It later falls back down as rain, but farmers are looking for rain for their crops on land, which brings us to the rotation of the earth that allows the wind to move water vapor over the earth and eventually over the farmers' land.

He draws up the drops of water, which distill as rain to the streams; the clouds pour down their moisture and abundant showers fall on mankind. Who can understand how he spreads out the clouds, how he thunders from his pavilion?

JOB 36:27-29

Thank you—Our Purposeful Designer—and Our God!

Such an intricate rain cycle is but another example of the complexities of design God created for man's benefit.

The vast oceans—71% of the earth's surface—is perfectly designed for initiation of the important Rain Cycle and just the right amount of rain each year!

More than 71% ocean would be a problem—too much rain and extreme floods.

Less than 71% ocean would also be a problem—not enough rain and so vast deserts!

And God said, "Let the water under the sky be gathered to one place, and let dry ground appear." And it was so. God called the dry ground "land," and the gathered waters he called "seas." And God saw that it was good. Then God said, "Let the land produce vegetation: seed-bearing plants and trees on the land that bear fruit with seeds in it, according to their various kinds." And it was so. The land produced vegetation: plants bearing seed according to their kinds and trees bearing fruit with seeds in it according to their kinds. And God saw that it was good. And there was evening, and there was morning— the third day.

GENESIS 1:9-13

The Third Day—Creation of the Dry Land and Vegetation

This passage declares the dramatic twofold work of God on the third day of creation:

- Dividing the water from the land

- Bringing forth the vegetation on the land

By the end of the third day of creation our Creator has constructed the land, the sky and the atmosphere, along with the water cycle of the oceans, all necessary for life to exist on earth. And once the contents were sculpted, God said, "Let the land produce vegetation."

(Genesis 1:11). And though science continues to search, to date they have found no other atmosphere in our universe that can support life—or vegetation.

The Importance of Vegetation and Plants to Humans

Our Purposeful Designer created more than 258,000 varieties of plants that have been discovered and named so far. And new varieties, even now, are continuing to be discovered!

Consider the Common Apple

- Vitamin C—prevents scurvy

- Fiber—fights digestive disorders, constipation, and dysentery

- Pectin—limits gall bladder and kidney problems

- Low sodium, high potassium—lowers blood pressure and fights heart disease

- Beneficial against peptic ulcers

"An Apple a Day Keeps the Doctor Away"

Ways in which plants are useful to you and me:

- As food—cereals, vegetables, fruits, nuts, herbs, edible flowers, cooking oils, sugar from beets and sugar cane

- Non-food products—wood for building, for burning, for cooking and heat, cloth for clothing, coal, soaps, paints, dyes

- Medicinal—coca plant as an anesthetic, coffee and tea as stimulants, kava kava as a tranquilizer, pineapple as an anti-inflammatory, poppy plant to produce codeine and morphine analgesic, quinine tree for an anti-malarial drug, thyme as a topical antifungal

- Aesthetic—wind breaks, providing privacy, ornamentals, lawn grasses, landscaping, a place for birds to nest

- For their beauty—your back yard, a beautiful flower, an arboretum, a pleasant hillside

- Others—many more including in literature and religion, state emblems, wreaths in memorials, in mythology

And God said, "Let there be lights in the expanse of the sky to separate the day from the night, and let them serve as signs to mark the seasons and days and years, and let them be lights in the expanse of the sky to give light on the earth." And it was so. God made two great lights—the greater light to govern the day and the lesser light to govern the night. He also made the stars. God set them in the expanse of the sky to give light on the earth, to govern the day and the night, and to separate light from darkness. And God saw that it was good. And there was evening, and there was morning—the fourth day.

GENESIS 1:14-19

CHAPTER 4

The Fourth Day
Creation of the Sun, Moon, and Stars

Those who are observant of the creation events find an interesting and sensible flow—the first three days are "preparation" while the next three days (days 4, 5, & 6) are the "filling". The preparation work included the creation of original light and the earth (Day 1); the sky and the water (Day 2); and the oceans, dry land, and vegetation (Day 3). The work was formative and foundational—geological work.

The second phase was the more detailed finishing or filling work.

Starting on Day 4, the heavens (created in Day 1) were populated with the sun, moon, and stars—each having useful work to do.

Then, on Day 5 birds and fish were created to populate the sky and water (created on Day 2).

To top everything off, on Day 6 living creatures, both animals and human beings, were created to populate the dry land and vegetation (created on Day 3).

The Sun's Rays and the Earth's Tilt: The Seasons Designed for Our Benefit

The special design of the "seasons" further shows our Purposeful Designer's love and concern for our wellbeing.

The pace of our year is set by the earth's rotation around the sun—and the fact that the earth's axis of spin is at a tilt of 23.5 degrees from the vertical—as the earth orbits the sun. The tilt means that during one half of the solar year (365 days, 5 hours, 48 minutes, and 46 seconds), our spot on the earth gets more sunlight and so the days are longer. During the other half of the year, our spot get less sunlight and so then the days are shorter.

The cycle of the "seasons" is important! And needful whether you live in the earth's Northern Hemisphere or the Southern Hemisphere:

- **Winter:** When the sun's rays are weak and the days shorter, in the cold of winter, plants are in a needed dormant rest period (some seeds won't germinate unless they go thru a cold period); bear hibernate and produce their young during the winter; and winter (with its killing freezes) protects much of the world's population from the advancement of tropical insects (which carry deadly diseases harmful to animals and humans.)

  The first day of winter, December 21, (the Winter Solstice) is the shortest day of sunlight in the northern hemisphere.

- **Spring:** With some more daylight in the spring—there is warming—and new life again; buds open into flowers; and animals get nourishing food again.

  The first day of spring, March 21, (the Vernal Equinox) is the time when the sun is shining directly over the earth's Equator.

- **Summer:** With more direct sun and longer days, there is the heat of the summer with more growth, fruit bearing and seed production. For we humans, it is a time for vacations, picnics, and swimming.

  The first day of summer, June 21, (the Summer Solstice) is the longest day of sunlight in the northern hemisphere.

- **Fall:** With the shortened days and cooling we get into fall—the shedding of leaves, birds migrate towards the warmer Equator—and animals and humans stock up for the coming winter ahead.

  The first day of fall, September 21, (the Autumnal Equinox) is again the time when the sun is shining directly over the earth's equator.

The heavens declare the glory of God; the skies proclaim the work of his hands.

PSALM 19:1

Lift up your eyes and look to the heavens: Who created all these? He who brings out the starry host one by one, he calls them each by name.

ISAIAH 40:26

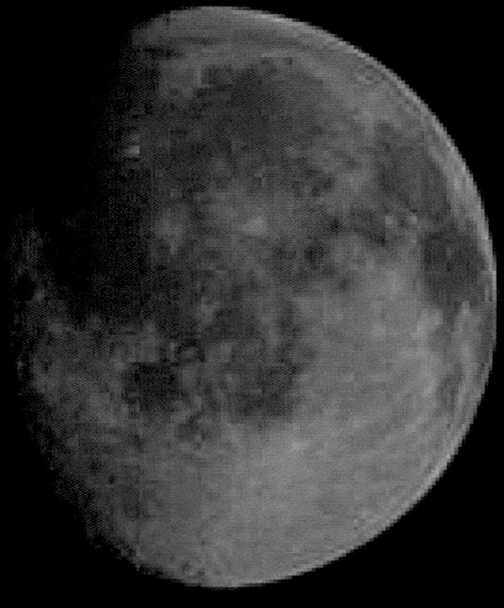

VERNAL EQUINOX
MARCH 21
First day of Spring
Sun over the Equator

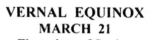
Washington, D.C.

EARTH

EQUATOR

Sunrise: 7:10 AM
Sunset: 7:21 PM
Sunlight: 12 hours, 11 minutes
50.8% of day in sunlight
43 degrees average March temperature

North of Arctic Circle
Sun will not set

TROPIC OF CANCER
Or the "Northern Tropic"
23°26'16" Latitude north of the Equator
The circle of latitude on the Earth that marks the most northerly position at which the Sun may appear directly overhead at its zenith (noon on June 21)

North of Arctic Circle
Sun will not rise

SUMMER SOLSTICE
JUNE 21
First day of Summer
Sun over Tropic of Cancer
Longest day of sunlight of the year

Washington, D.C.

EARTH

Tropic of Cancer

EQUATOR

Sunrise: 5:43 AM
Sunset: 8:37 PM
Sunlight: 14 hours, 54 minutes
62.1% of day in sunlight
71 degrees average June temperature

SUN

Washington, D.C.

EQUATOR

Tropic of Capricorn

EARTH

WINTER SOLSTICE
DECEMBER 21
First day of Winter
Sun over Tropic of Capricorn
Shortest day of sunlight of the year

Sunrise: 7:23 AM
Sunset: 4:49 PM
Sunlight: 9 hours, 23 minutes
39.3% of day in sunlight
36 degrees average December temperature

TROPIC OF CAPRICORN
Or the "Southern Tropic"
23°26'16" Latitude south of the Equator
The circle of latitude on the Earth that marks the most southerly position at which the Sun may appear directly overhead at its zenith (noon on December 21)

The Cause of the Climate in Washington, D.C.

(38 degrees North Latitude)

Tilt of 23.5%
from the vertical

EQUATOR

EARTH

AUTUMNAL EQUINOX
SEPTEMBER 21
First day of Fall
Sun over the Equator

Sunrise: 6:55 AM
Sunset: 7:07 PM
Sunlight: 12 hours, 12 minutes
50.8% of day in sunlight
67 degrees average September temperature

Sunrise/Sunset over Washington, D.C.

The earth orbits the sun at a constant speed; the distance from the sun is unchanging; the 23 and ½ degree tilt remains the same; and the earth makes one complete rotation on its axis in an unchanging 23 hours, 56 minutes, and 4 seconds. The cycle of the earth's orbit around the sun is unchanging—taking 365 days, 5 hours, 48 minutes, and 46 seconds. Incredible!

Year after year, because of the unchanging precision of the universe—the sun rise and sets—at the same precise time as the year before—for any location on the earth that you can name.

For instance, at Washington, D.C., at September 21st, the sun rises at the same time each year—6:54 AM. The sun sets at the same time each year—7:07 PM. Daylight is always 12 hours and 13 minutes. *There is a give-and-take of two or three minutes.*

Your computer can give you a printout (www.gaisma.com) of the sunrise and sunset times at any day for any location on the earth. Discontinuity in the chart times occurs when we move to Daylight Savings Time on March 10th and when we move to Standard Time on November 3rd.

The First Day of Fall in Washington, DC: Sept. 21			
Year	Sunrise	Sunset	Daylight
1970	6:54	7:09	12:15
1980	6:55	7:08	12:13
1990	6:54	7:09	12:15
2000	6:55	7:08	12:13
2001	6:55	7:08	12:13
2002	6:54	7:08	12:14
2003	6:54	7:09	12:15
2004	6:55	7:08	12:13
2005	6:55	7:08	12:13
2006	6:54	7:08	12:14
2007	6:54	7:09	12:15
2008	6:54	7:07	12:13
2009	6:54	7:07	12:13
2010	6:54	7:08	12:14
2011	6:54	7:08	12:14
2012	6:54	7:07	12:13
2013	6:55	7:08	12:13
2014	6:54	7:08	12:14
2015	6:54	7:09	12:15
2020	6:55	7:07	12:12
2030	6:55	7:08	12:13
2040	6:55	7:07	12:12
2050	6:55	7:08	12:13

Sunrise/Sunset: Washington, D.C.
Latitude 38° North; www. gaisma.com

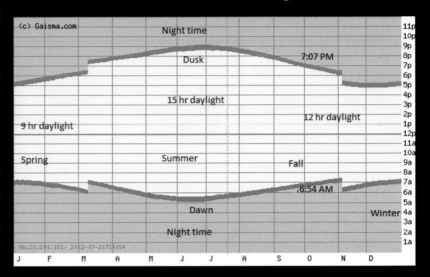

The First Day of Fall in Washington, DC : Sept. 21

	2008	2009	2010	2011	2012
Sunrise (AM)	6:54	6:54	6:54	6:54	6:54
Sunset (PM)	7:07	7:07	7:08	7:08	7:07
Daylight	12 hrs 13 min	12 hrs 13 min	12 hrs 14 min	12 hrs 14 min	12 hrs 13 min

Our Creator Set It Perfectly At 23 and ½ Degrees!

God got it perfectly correct when He designed the seasons for us by setting the 23 and ½ degrees tilt of the earth's spin axis.

Perfection at 23 and ½ tilt of the spin axis: But for sure, our Purposeful Designer worked it out in a complicated fashion—for the benefit of all his creation. We would have our seasons, and they would be bearable and even enjoyable as they are now.

The Sun's Rays and the Earth's Tilt: Seasons Designed for our Benefit

Caused by earth's 23.5° tilt on its axis from vertical—changing the Sun's rays in how direct they hit the earth's landscape—from month to month.

- Winter—plants in dormant rest period

- Spring—new life, buds open into flowers

- Summer—growth, reproduction, seeds

- Fall—shedding of leaves and seeds

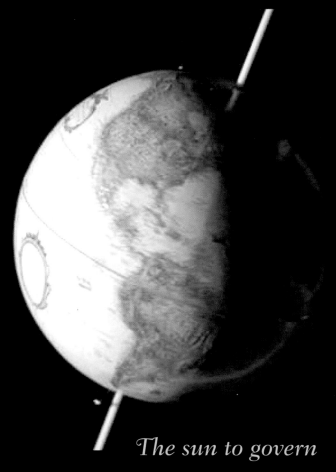

The sun to govern the day, His love endures forever.

PSALM 136:8

What If? By Chance...it was a 0° tilt?

With 0 degrees tilt of the spin axis: What do you think would happen if the earth's axis of spin was say 0 degrees from the vertical? With 12 hours daylight and 12 hours night, every day of the year, we all would have no "seasons": it would be boring; bears would not hibernate; birds would not migrate; seeds would not germinate; there would be little "variety in life"; and worse—mortality rates would go through the roof because of insect infestations.

Or it was a 50° tilt?

With 50 degrees tilt of the spin axis: What do you think would happen if the earth's axis was say 50 degrees from the vertical? The extreme portions of the earth's hemispheres would get extreme "seasons" with daylight and the heat of the sun 24 hours a day for up to half of the year. The other half of the year some would see no daylight or heat of the sun 24 hours a day. *There would be no life as we know it now!*

At winter time in Alaska there would be no daylight at all as the sun would not shine on Alaska.

At summer time in Alaska there would be no darkness—no nighttime—as the sun would shine on Alaska all day long.

Alaska winter

Then and Now:
Use of the Preciseness of the Sunrise

Stonehenge, England

The prehistoric site of Stonehenge, England displays the intelligence of our ancient ancestors 4,000 years ago! They knew of the preciseness of the earth's and sun's circuit and devised a complicated time-piece knowing that things repeated year after year. One of the uses of the Stonehenge site was to tell of an early harvest time which they called "Summer Solstice". When the sunrise (about 4:30 AM) as seen from the

Heel Stone, shown perfectly through one certain Trilithon of rocks—it marked the Summer Solstice—June 21—a religious celebration time—and to predict when some planting and harvesting was to be done.

Incredibly, the ancients at Stonehenge had numerous other uses for the Stonehenge "timepiece", well documented in Gerald Hawkins' book, "Stonehenge Decoded", published in 1965.

"Ground Zero" Memorial Designs

Yes, year after year, our earth orbits the sun in a precise and repeatable way! Here are modern day designs of the earth and sun working together—"like clockwork".

The designers of the September 11, 2001 ground zero tragedy memorial utilized the sun's preciseness. Some designs have skylight openings precisely positioned such that a ray of sunlight shines down to the memorial below for about 1½ hours in the morning on only one day a year—September 11— and at the time 8:46 AM till 10:28 AM—the time of the terrorist attacks on the U.S. World Trade Center.

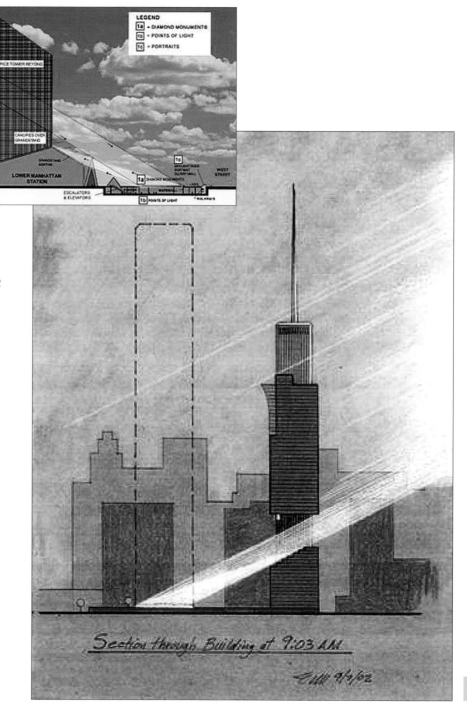

Section through Building at 9:03 AM

The Many Benefits of our Moon

The moon gives us light—and beauty—at night. And, our moon acts as a bit of a "time piece" itself, as it orbits our earth in precisely 27.3217 days—called the "Lunar Month". Animals and humans use its "phases" to "tell time". It's for all our benefit! American Indians, for instance, referred to "Many Moons"— counting from full moon to full moon. Also, the interaction of the moon and our earth's rotation causes the ocean's tides.

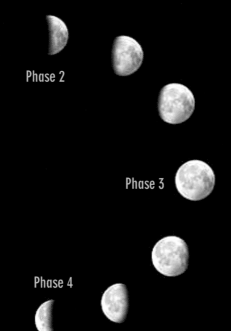

Phase 2

Phase 1

Phase 3

Phase 4

The Phases of the Moon

Phase 1: New Moon—darkened phase: When the moon is between the sun and the earth, sunlight doesn't fall on the portion of the moon facing the earth. Astronomers call this darkened phase a *new moon*. The night

Phase 2: First Quarter—half moon: As the moon orbits our earth, after about seven days, we can see half a full moon, commonly called a *half moon*. This phase is known as the first quarter, because it occurs one-quarter of the way through the month-long cycle.

Phase 3: Full Moon—entire sunlit moon in view: About seven days later, the moon is on the side of the earth opposite the sun. The entire sunlit side of the moon is visible to us (we see a beautiful sight and the *Man in the Moon*), and this phase is called the *full moon*.

Phase 4: Last Quarter—half moon in view again: Then about seven days from the full moon, we see a half moon, again. This is called the *last quarter*.

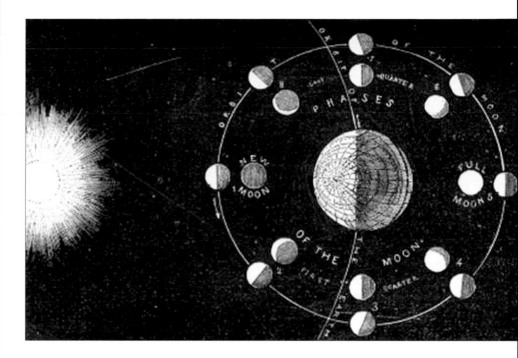

After another approximately seven days the Lunar Month is completed, as the moon is between the earth and sun, again, producing another new moon—back to phase 1.

The Beneficial Ocean Tides:
Our Moon's Gravitational Pull Produces the Ocean Tides

Because the earth makes one full rotation in approximately twenty-four hours, there is a tidal gravitational pull (caused by the moon) every twelve hours at the near side of the moon (near tidal bulge) and also a bulge on the far side of the earth (a far tidal bulge). Likewise there are low tides in between, at time lapses of six hours, between the two high tides.

The constant ebb and flow of tidal waters accounts for constant changes in our shoreline and marshlands. The tides impact the availability and delivery of important plant and chemical nutrients, thereby replenishing our earth's wetlands—*keeping them alive.*

The tidal rhythm of the seas is dependable, predictable, and critical to the good health of our planet—set in motion by our Purposeful Designer.

As the chart on the following page shows, at the ocean's edge, roughly speaking, we get a high tide every 12 hours—and get a low tide every 12 hours.

1. 12 midn—high tide (A)

   3 am—mid tide

2. 6 am—low tide

   9 am—mid tide

3. 12 noon—high tide (B)

   3pm—mid tide

4. 6 pm—low tide

   9 pm—mid tide

5. 12 midn—high tide (A)

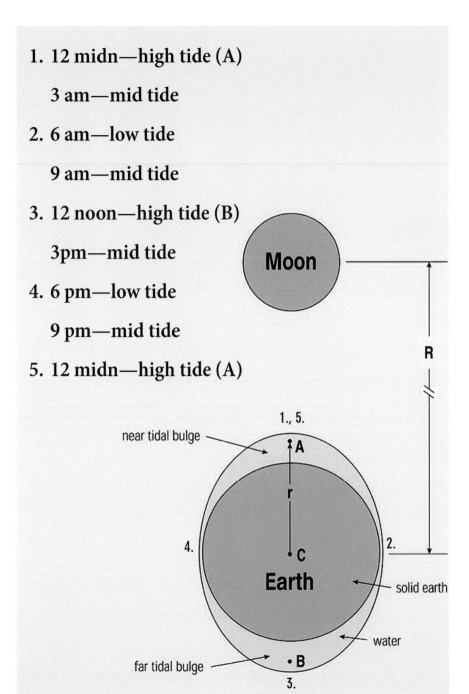

1. **At point A on the chart**, (12 midnight), the moon is "pulling" on the water causing a high tide (near tidal bulge). In a sympathetic move, at point B, opposite, there is also another bulge, another high tide (far tidal bulge).

2. **After the earth takes 6 hours** to rotate 90 degrees, (6 AM), there is no moon pull, and a low tide.

3. **Another 6 hours** of earth rotation of 90 degrees, (12 noon), and you get a high tide again—(this is point B—the far tidal bulge).

4. **Another 6 hours** of rotation (6 PM), and you get a low tide again

5. **Another 6 hours** of rotation (12 midnight—24 hours total) and we are back to high tide again (point A).

43

More on the Tides

Now the previous graphic that showed the tide cycle repeating every 24 ours is accurate ROUGHLY SPEAKING. But, the earth doesn't make one complete rotation in exactly 24 hours. Actually it takes 23 hours, 53 minutes, and 4 seconds (constant, not changing). Also, since the moon moves around the earth, it is not always in the same place at the same time of day. *So, each day, the times for the low and high tides changes by approximately 45 minutes.*

On the Tide Table, which is just typical, you can see that March 2nd the morning high tide doesn't come precisely 24 hours after the high tide of March 1st. AM high tide of March 1st is 5:35 AM and the AM high tide of March 2nd is at 6:20 AM. It is 45 minutes later. Also, the afternoon high tides are not exactly 12 hours after the morning high tides.

So we need to calculate the times of the tides, which are predictable, in Tide Tables, and this makes the activities of fishermen and navigators ever so much more successful!

Thanks to our very Purposeful Designer!

(Tides vary dramatically based on a location's latitude, the topography, varying distance of the earth to the moon, and even the phase of the moon.)

TIDE TABLE

MARCH		High				Low	
		AM	HT	PM	HT	AM	PM
1	Tue	5:35	5.3	5:43	4.8	11:42	11:58
2	Wed	6:20	5.4	6:28	5.0		12:26
3	Thu	7:01	5.4	7:09	5.2	12:43	1:06
4	Fri ●	7:38	5.4	7:47	5.3	1:24	1:43
5	Sat	8:14	5.3	8:22	5.4	2:02	2:17
6	Sun	8:48	5.1	8:56	5.4	2:39	2:50
7	Mon	9:20	5.0	9:28	5.3	3:14	3:22
8	Tue	9:52	4.7	10:01	5.3	3:49	3:54
9	Wed	10:24	4.6	10:36	5.2	4:25	4:30
10	Thu	11:00	4.4	11:18	5.1	5:05	5:10
11	Fri	11:43	4.3			5:51	5:57
12	Sat ◑	12:08	5.1	12:37	4.2	6:46	6:54
13	Sun	1:09	5.1	2:42	4.3	8:48	8:59
14	Mon	3:16	5.2	3:51	4.4	9:55	10:07
15	Tue	4:24	5.4	4:58	4.8	10:58	11:13
16	Wed	5:28	5.6	6:00	5.3	11:56	
17	Thu	6:27	5.9	6:57	5.7	12:15	12:49
18	Fri	7:21	6.1	7:51	6.2	1:12	1:39
19	Sat ○	8:13	6.1	8:44	6.5	2:07	2:28
20	Sun	9:03	6.1	9:35	6.7	3:00	3:16
21	Mon	9:52	5.9	10:26	6.6	3:52	4:04
22	Tue	10:42	5.7	11:19	6.4	4:45	4:53
23	Wed	11:34	5.3			5:38	5:44
24	Thu	12:14	6.1	12:28	5.0	6:33	6:38
25	Fri	1:12	5.8	1:26	4.8	7:30	7:37
26	Sat ◐	2:13	5.5	2:27	4.6	8:30	8:40
27	Sun	3:16	5.2	3:30	4.6	9:30	9:46
28	Mon	4:16	5.1	4:30	4.6	10:28	10:48
29	Tue	5:11	5.1	5:26	4.8	11:21	11:44
30	Wed	6:01	5.1	6:15	5.1		12:08
31	Thu	6:46	5.2	7:00	5.3	12:34	12:51

The Leatherback Turtle Takes Advantage of the Ocean's Tides

One of the many creatures that take advantage of the tide is the Leatherback Turtle. The Leatherback Turtle generally stays in the ocean, but when the tide is extra high, the female comes inland to lay her eggs—above the level where ocean water can harmfully inundate them. Upon hatching, the young ones have a short crawl back to the water and safety.

What If ? ...

What if our tides were not perfectly designed by God, as they are now—the moon a perfect size and distance away from earth for the *just right* gravitational pull and tides?

What if the moon was much larger or a distance closer to the earth? Humans on earth would be doomed because the too great gravitational force of the moon would make the tides huge—*and devastating!*

What if the moon was much smaller or a distance farther from the earth? The ocean's tides would be insignificant— *and of no benefit at all to mankind.*

He also
made
the stars.

48

What we see in the night sky

The moon, some of the planets, and some star constellations—such as Ursa Minor, Ursa Major, Cassiopeia, and Draco—all revolve around the North Star every twenty-four hours. (Pictorial shows the Hubble Space Telescope)

Stars

We actually can't see all the stars, but, the stars in our Milky Way Galaxy all appear, from the surface of the earth, to revolve around what we call the North Star—every 24 hours. Isn't that handy! Purposefully designed. That situation helps us know where we are at night—and, for celestial navigation.

The Number of Stars in the Heavens

Greek astronomer Ptolemy figured he could see 3,000 stars with the naked eye.

In the 17th Century, Galileo with the newly invented telescope, figured it was in the millions.

Recently, in the year 2010, a Yale astronomer with the help of a powerful telescope in Hawaii, speculated that the number of galaxies and the number of stars in each galaxy could be 500 billion in each case. Multiply this out and you get in the range of one thousand trillion stars—(that's 10 with 23 zeros)!

Stars Useful in Celestial Navigation

When a ship's captain wants to measure its latitude during the night he uses a sextant sighting on Polaris, the North Star, which, when seen from the Northern Hemisphere, always stays within one degree of the celestial North Pole.

Standing at the North Pole, aiming your sextant at Polaris, you read 90° from level earth—hence we read latitude 90° North at the North Pole. In like manner, standing on the equator, aiming your sextant at Polaris, you read zero° from level earth—hence we read zero° latitude at the equator.

There is more to celestial navigation, and it is actually quite a complex process. Nowadays, God has given us GPS (global positioning system) technology—and we all use it. However, the sextant and celestial navigation continues to be used by private yachtsmen, and particularly by long-distance cruising yachts voyaging around the globe.

Sailor's Sextant

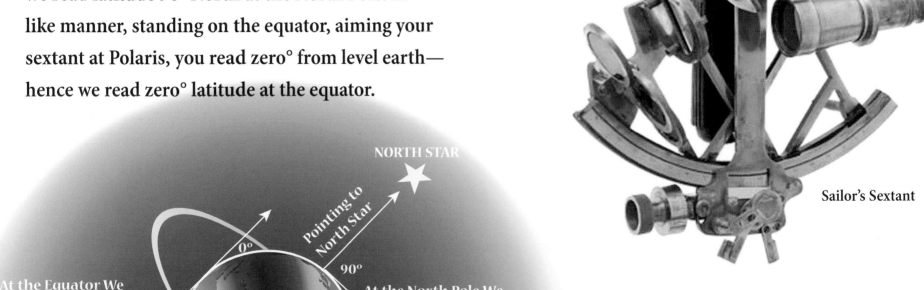

NORTH STAR

Pointing to North Star

0°

90°

At the Equator We Read "Latitude 0° North"

At the North Pole We Read "Latitude 90° North"

Some say that the number of stars in the sky is as countless as the number of grains of sand on our seashore. And, one estimate of the number of grains of sand on our seashores is 10 with 24 zeros! Yes, "He also made the stars."

The X Structure and the Cross of Jesus

Scientists are learning more all the time about the stars in our heavens. In fact, astronomers recently discovered (with the help of the Hubble Telescope) the Whirlpool Galaxy—31 million light years away.

Looking closely at it, they call it the "X-Structure"!

We like to say, God is reminding us of his Son—Jesus Christ.

Yes, the first Adam was created per Genesis. The second Adam is Jesus Christ who paid for the sins of you and me on the cross 2,000 years ago.

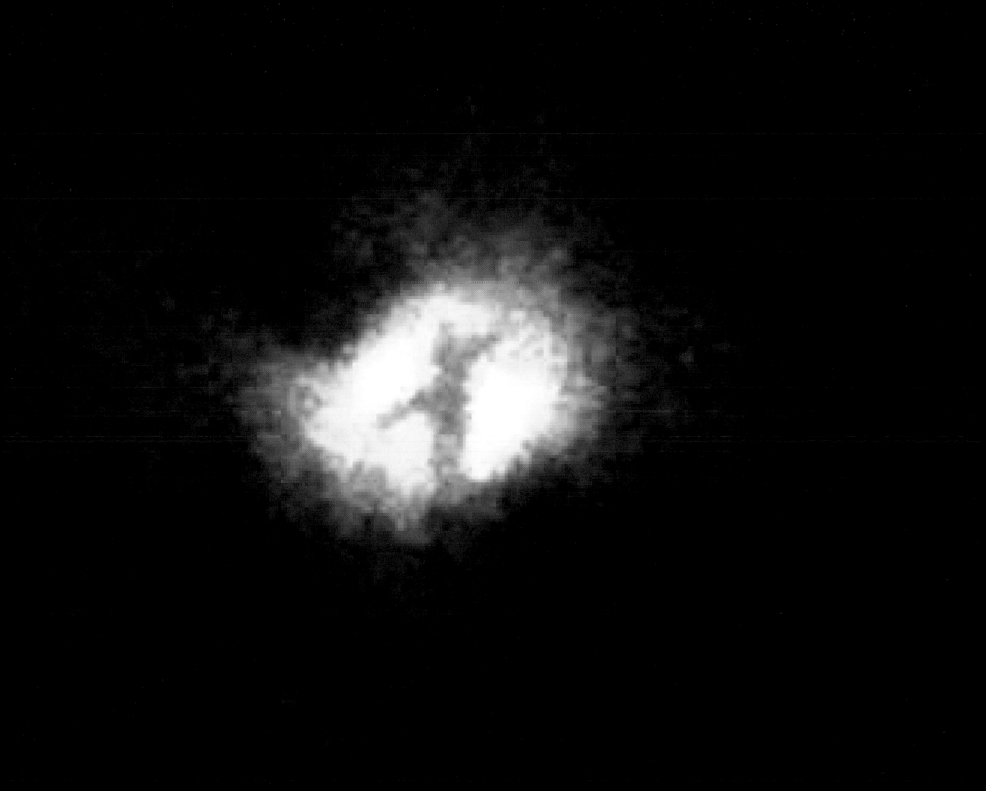

And God said, "Let the waters teem with living creatures, and let birds fly above the earth across the expanse of the sky." So God created the great creatures of the sea and every living and moving thing with which the water teems according to their kinds, and every win ged bird according to its kind. And God saw that it was good. God blessed them and said, "Be fruitful and increase in number and fill the water in the seas, and let the birds increase on the earth." And there was evening, and there was morning—the fifth day.

GENESIS 1:20-23

CHAPTER 5

The Fifth Day
Creation of the Birds and Fish

Why the Birds and Fish Were Created

To add to the big picture of the earth: *To let birds fly above the earth, and fish to fill the water in the seas.*

- Birds and fish clean up the earth: Vultures clean the land; catfish clean the ocean floor.

- Birds and fish are part of the *food chain*: Birds and animals eat fish; we humans eat birds and fish.

- They add beauty and interest to life: For instance, the herons and egrets are beautiful; the eagles are awesome.

- General sports activity for humans: Many enjoy the sport of fishing, bird watching, and bird hunting.

"Instincts" Preprogrammed by
Our Intelligent and Purposeful Designer

Instinct

"Instinct", created by our Purposeful Designer, is among the many miracles of nature not easily explained by present day science. It is present in almost all living creatures.

Webster's Definition of "Instinct":

- *A natural or inherent aptitude or capacity.*

- *A largely inheritable and unalterable tendency by an organism to make a complex and specific response to environmental stimuli without involving reason.*

- *Behavior that is mediated by reactions below the conscious level.*

The Instincts of Birds

Many species of birds migrate to take advantage of warmer seasonal temperatures, which offers them a greater availability of food sources and breeding. They use various methods to navigate during migration including the sun by day and the stars at night. In some species these are backed up (such as during cloudy conditions) by the ability to sense the earth's geomagnetic fields through photoreceptors.

Birds are often marked by scientists so their migrations may be tracked and studied. And while we are amazed that adult birds never fail to find their way, we find it even more remarkable when such feats are accomplished by inexperienced young birds. As strange as it may seem, many shore birds fly south before their young are mature enough to make the trip. A few weeks later, young birds that have never left the nesting area, fly in a perfectly straight line to meet their elders at the wintering grounds.

The Instincts of Salmon

The young salmon spends his first several months of life in the streams of Alaska and Canada where his life began. Soon afterward he will migrate to the southerly salt water of the Pacific Ocean where he will spend several years growing to adulthood in the food-rich waters of the ocean before he instinctively know it's time to return to the place of his origin to breed.

Guided largely by the sense of smell, he will swim thousands of miles back to his birthplace, overcoming rapids and other treacherous obstacles. Once at his destination, the male will battle for the right to fertilize the female's eggs, and the female will batter her body as she digs a ditch where she will lay her eggs. Both the male and female will soon die from sheer exhaustion. In time, the eggs will hatch, and a new generation of tiny salmon will once again begin their cycle of life.

"Many instincts are so wonderful that their development will probably appear to a reader a difficulty sufficient to overthrow my whole Evolution theory."

CHARLES DARWIN,
Origin of Species, Chapter VIII, 1988,
New York University

Have You Wondered How Fish Swim?

Fish propel themselves by alternately contracting paired sets of muscles located on both sides of their backbones. Such contractions result in S-shaped curves that, upon reaching the back fin, apply backward force on the water, moving the fish forward. Fins also increase the tail's surface area, increasing the speed at which a fish swims. Its streamlined body design lowers water friction. Some fish have a swim bladder to help them manipulate gases to adjust their buoyancy.

We Learn from the Creator

The modern submarine, like so many other designs these days, takes its cue from the Creator to achieve the best result:

- It has "fins" that gives it stabilization.

- It is shaped like a fish—streamlined for speed.

- It has "bladders" that take on water to adjust its buoyancy and so its depth in the water.

- It has "sonar" which some fish use for "seeing".

Why Does Ice Float?

Have you ever wondered why ice floats?

In order to save the fish is one reason.

If ice was to sink instead of floating, life on our earth would be far different! Rivers and lakes would freeze from the bottom up, causing them to completely freeze over with ice, making life difficult if not impossible for aquatic animals. Instead, ice forms on top of the water and floats, acting as an insulator to keep the deeper water from freezing even at the most frigid temperatures above ground.

As a rule, a substance floats if it is less dense (or has less mass per unit volume) than other components of a mixture; it sinks if it is more dense (or has more mass per unit volume) than other components of a mixture. When most elements solidify (*freeze*), they become denser than they were in the liquid state and their increased mass or weight causes them to sink.

The Why:

- To make insulation so water below doesn't freeze

- So fish don't freeze

- Winter transportation across frozen lakes

- To allow harvesting ice in winter for "ice boxes" to preserve food

But our Purposeful Designer caused frozen water to miraculously defy that rule in accordance with His master plan! Water (H_2O) differs from other substances because of "hydrogen bonding". So, as water cools to "freezing", the hydrogen bonds adjust to hold the negatively charged oxygen atoms apart. This produces a crystalline lattice known as "ice" that expands. In that condition, it is actually less dense and lighter than liquid water—so it floats.

The frozen ice at the surface insulates the water below (keeping it from freezing)—so the fish don't freeze, but survive through the cold northern winters.

Our Purposeful Designer Has a Sense of Humor

Many marvel and enjoy what we call God's sense of humor! Some animals that we smile at include the penguin and the koala bear.

Many in the oceans look weird and somewhat humorous including our little friend here—the Piglet Squid.

- The "Piglet Squid" the size of an avocado

- Two eyes, a large nose, a smiling mouth, gargantuan eyebrowns, and fat like a piglet

- Cute to see but probably not edible

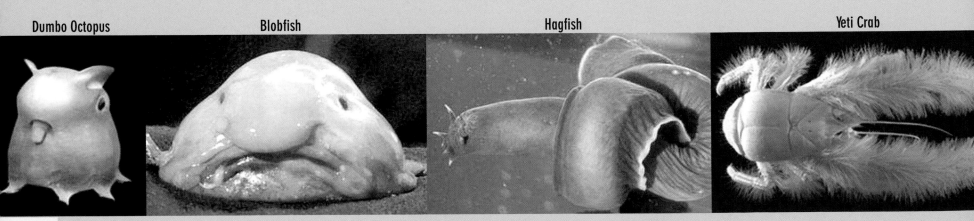

Dumbo Octopus | Blobfish | Hagfish | Yeti Crab

*Do you agree—the five words in Genesis—
"He also made the stars" as an
understatement—and humorous?*

And God said, "Let the land produce living creatures according to their kinds: livestock, creatures that move along the ground, and wild animals, each according to its kind." And it was so. God made the wild animals according to their kinds, the livestock according to their kinds, and all the creatures that move along the ground according to their kinds. And God saw that it was good. Then God said, "Let us make man in our own image, in our likeness, and let them rule over the fish of the sea and the birds of the air, over the livestock, over the earth, and over the creatures that move along the ground."

So God created man in his own image, in the image of God he created him; male and female he created them. God blessed them and said to them, "Be fruitful and increase in number; fill the earth and subdue it. Rule over the fish of the sea and the birds of the air and over every living creature that moves on the ground." Then God said, "I give you every seed-bearing plant on the face of the whole earth and every tree that has fruit with seed in it. They will be yours for food. And to all the beasts of the earth and to all the birds of the air and all the creatures that move on the ground—everything that has the breath of life in it—I give every green plant for food." And it was so. God saw all that he had made, and it was very good. And there was evening, and there was morning—the sixth day.

GENESIS 1:24-31

CHAPTER 6

Creation Day Six
Creation of Land Creatures and Humans

God Made Domestic Animals for Us

Because of his great love for us, God purposefully created many types of domestic animals for our use—per the list below—from the camel to the water buffalo.

- Camel
- Cat
- Chicken
- Cow
- Dog
- Donkey
- Goose
- Horse
- Pig
- Pigeon
- Rabbit
- Sheep
- Silkworm
- Turkey
- Water Buffalo

65

The Amazing Camel

After creating the desert, God designed the camel for the benefit of those humans making their home in those arid lands. Although the human being is not specifically designed for desert climate, the camel was and is therefore very useful to man. Used as a beast of burden and for transportation, it can carry amazingly large loads under very dry, hot conditions for days on end. How can the camel do this?

Designed for all kinds of difficult desert conditions, the camel has a "hump" which is made up of a large mass of fat that is a food reserve allowing the camel to go for days without eating.

More importantly, the camel is designed with extensive water storage capabilities allowing it to endure weeks without drinking water. A design wonder, one of the camel's stomach chambers is built to hold a large quantity of water— up to thirty gallons (which it can initially consume in as little as ten minutes). Mankind

have their smaller water canteens for hydration during desert work; but, you can say that the amazing camel has the largest canteen of all— at 30 gallons!

For carrying large loads, the camel is equipped with a strong body and large wide hoofs so it doesn't sink into the sand during its travels.

God also designed the camel to operate at an amazingly high internal body temperature—up to 106 degrees with no ill effects.

The camel also provides its human keeper with milk and meat.

The Creator thought of everything!

- Designed to help humans in desert operations
- Has hump to store fat for a reserve of food
- Stomach has built-in canteen of 30 gal of water
- Has huge hooves for efficient desert traveling
- Can operate at 106° internal body temperature
- Provides milk and meat to humans

Cattle and Cows

The cow is specially designed to eat and digest the very abundant grass given to us on this earth for nourishment. This is because it was designed with four efficient stomach chambers to get the total job done. Of course the cow is quite useful to us—producing 15 gallons of milk per day (in two separate milking sessions). The cow is not only very useful but amazing in what it can do. Cows and cattle are easily domesticated and can thrive in all kinds of environments. Living on grassland, the cow can get its life-giving energy from raw grass—a cellulose substance—that humans cannot digest, because of the special design of its complicated and remarkable digestive system.

The cow's stomach is a complex organ divided into four chambers. The first stomach is called the rumen which receives the grass or hay. There it stays and ferments for a few days—aided by bacteria—while being converted to simple sugars. Soon the mixture moves to the second chamber where it is combined with enzyme-saturated liquid. When the cow has the leisure to "ruminate," it will regurgitate the soggy mixture out of the second stomach; then will more finely chew it before swallowing the mixture again. After swallowing again, the mixture, now called "cud," re-enters the second stomach to go through a filtering process. The largely liquid mixture moves to the third stomach called the "omasum" where more digestion and refining takes place. The thoroughly refined food passes to the fourth stomach which

- Can eat and digest grass

- Has four stomach chambers

- Provides many things for us: milk, meat, hide, bones for gelatin, fertilizer

secretes strong acids and enzymes, completing the digestive process.

The dairy cow continuously produces milk—not only for its offspring but also for human consumption—giving the farmer up to 15 gallons of milk per day—which can be made into butter, cheese, and ice cream. Nearly every part of a cow is eventually used by man: milk for drinking, meat for food, hide for leather, bones and hooves for gelatin and glue, and manure for fertilizer.

Cuts of Meat we use from a Steer

Mostly we use the female for the milk and the male (a neutered male is called a steer) for its meat. The cuts of meat a butcher produces include: brisket, chuck & blade, flank, leg, neck & clod, ribs, rump, silverside, sirloin, and topside. Be assured that most of this ends up in hamburger. About 95% of a steer is ultimately used by humans.

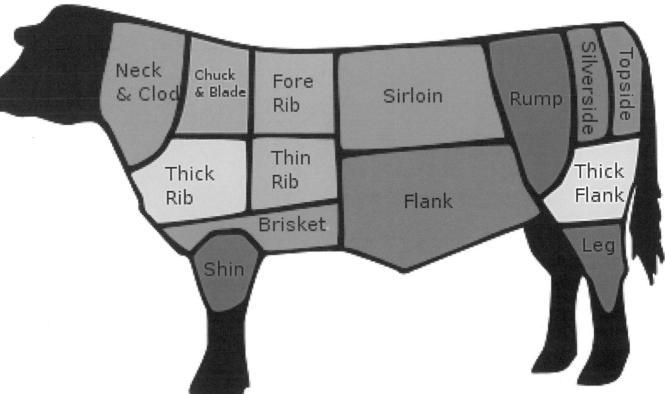

*So God created man
in his own image,
in the image of God
he created him; male and
female he created them.*

GENESIS 1:27

The Amazing Uniqueness of the Human Being

As said in the Bible, we are "created in the image of God", which is hard to understand—we realize. But, what has been designed into us—we should be thankful for:

- Intellect and Will

- Abstract thinking skill

- Communication Skills

- Able to Question

- We can Show Emotions

- We can Show Creativity

- God has given us a Moral Consciousness

- Most importantly, we have been created with a God Consciousness

That is, inwardly, we know that we were reverently created by something greater than us!

God's Design of our Remarkable Body

Your human body is composed of hundreds of trillions of cells. Recent science (since 1950), has shown the immense complexity of cells and molecules as they go about doing their jobs. "Molecular machines" haul cargo from one place in the cell to another along "highways" made of other molecules, while still others act to hold the cell in shape. These machines are able to turn cellular switches on and off, sometimes killing the cell (hopefully—a "bad" one) or causing it to grow. Solar powered machines capture the energy of photons and store it in chemicals. Electrical machines allow current to flow through nerves. Manufacturing machines build other molecular machines, as well as themselves. Cells swim using machines, copy themselves with machinery, and ingest food with machinery. In short, highly sophisticated molecular machines control every cellular process. Thus the details of your life are finely calibrated, and the machinery of life—in your body—is enormously complex.

And everything that was created— was created for a purpose.

A Purpose for Everything, Including the Appendix

Yes, there IS a purpose for everything, including the human appendix which was once thought of as useless or a "vestigial appendage". Doctors now know that the appendix is actually a "safe house" for beneficial bacteria in the human gut. You get your appendix removed only when absolutely necessary!

Blood Clotting

And, you never stopped to consider how complex a supposedly straightforward thing as your "blood clotting" really is. When a person or animal suffers a cut it normally bleeds for only a short time before a clot stops the flow; the clot eventually hardens, and the cut heals over. In fact, blood clot formation is so familiar we seldom give it much thought. However, biochemical investigation has shown that clotting is a very complex and miraculous process involving a score of interdependent components. The absence of any of these components causes—continuation of the bleeding.

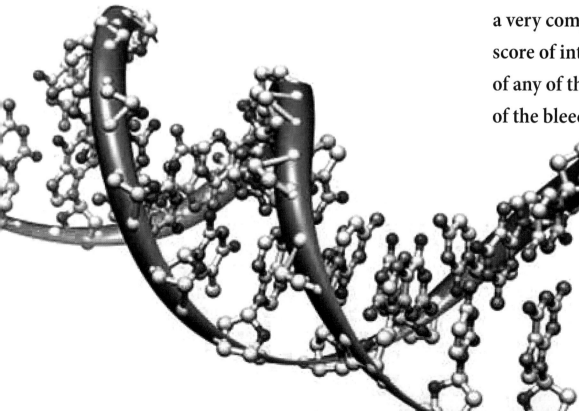

For the life of the creature is in the blood.

LEVITICUS 17:11

Mother's Milk

Nestlé Incorporated, the developer of infant formula for young babies—"supports breastfeeding and believes that breast milk is the best start a baby can have in life." "Infants should be exclusively breastfed for the first six months of life to achieve optimal growth, development, and health—"

Mother's milk which is loaded with antibodies, protects infants from allergies and illness in their early days. As the baby continues to nurse (and the baby gains in weight) the mother's milk increases in its fat content so the babies hunger is more quickly satisfied.

The Cell—Not a Bit of Slime

Our Understanding of the Human Cell has been a Progression.

- **1859:** Charles Darwin dubbed it "slime"

- **1900's:** Cell thought of as a "lump of carbon"

- **1995:** The microscope saw atoms in cells

- **2003:** The sequencing of human DNA completed

- **Now:** We now find each cell is incredibly complex, like a fully active and organized city, doing jobs necessary for our being and well being!

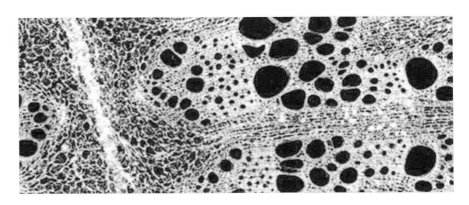

There are 17 MILLION bits of information in one human cell, and there are more than 250 genes in each cell.

Here is a sketch produced by Roche Drug Company that they call "Biomedical Pathways, Metabolic Pathways, Pathway 1b, Biochem Zone G5, Human Cell".

But, wait! That is just one hundredth of all that is going on in that one metabolic cell of yours. The total view shows all the activity, with the detail of the earlier sketch below just a small segment. The chart of the total view is displayed by Roche on a large wall—in a large room!

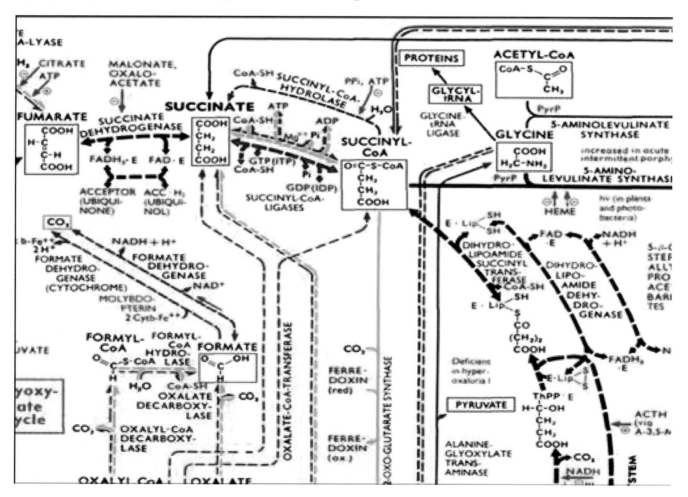

The Perfect Design of the Human head

Not only intelligent design but also purposeful design (for us) went into the result of your incredible human head!

The Brain and Skull

Because the brain is your body's miraculous central processor, it must be located where it would suffer minimal abuse—and be surrounded by a hard bony substance, called the skull or cranium, to protect it. It accommodates connections from all over the body for the flow of blood and the passage of vital electrical impulses that control everything from breathing and heartbeat to logical thinking processes and problem solving.

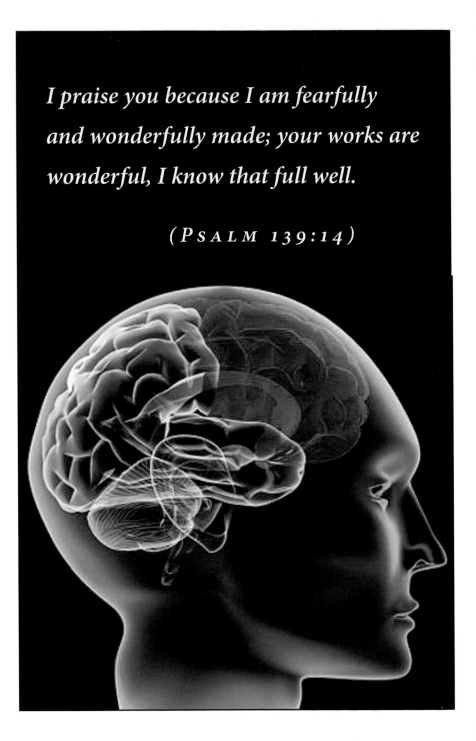

I praise you because I am fearfully and wonderfully made; your works are wonderful, I know that full well.

(PSALM 139:14)

The Perfect Design of the Head

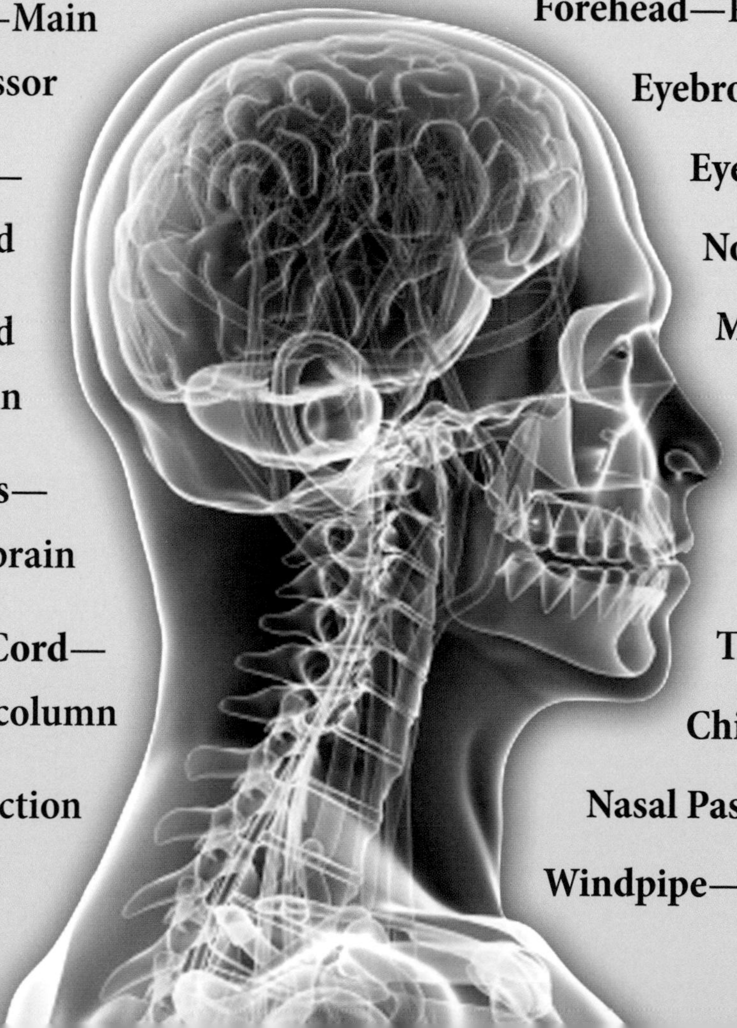

Hair—To protect the scalp

Brain—Main central processor

Ear Lobes— Face forward

Ears—High up and close to the brain

Blood Vessels— To and from brain

Spinal Cord— Protected by spinal column

Skin—For protection

Scull/Scalp—To protect the brain

Forehead—Protects eyes

Eyebrows—To protect the eye

Eyes—High up and close to brain

Nose—Set above the mouth

Mouth—Opening for food, air, talk

Tongue—Moves food to throat

Lips—Doors to the mouth

Teeth—To chew food

Throat—Connects mouth to food pipe

Chin—Lowermost part of face

Nasal Passage—Conditions air

Windpipe—Connects voicebox to lungs

The Eyes

Our two eyes (the two for depth perception) are located high on the head for best viewing. They are recessed and have eyebrows for further protection. Their design includes a blinking mechanism and tears to keep them moist, as well as an iris, which, like a camera aperture opens and closes the pupil depending on the light around it. Light passes through the pupil, lens and cornea before reaching the retina, which like the receiver in a video camera processes the images generating electrical impulses that move to the brain via the optic nerve.

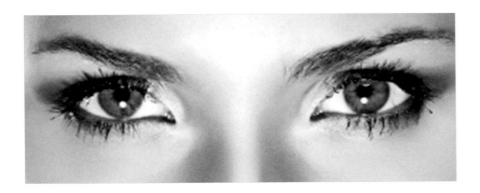

The Nose

The nose is located right above the mouth so as to best gauge scent (either good or bad) of food being taken into the mouth. High in the nasal cavity a million tiny sensory (olfactory) receptors are concentrated in a tiny patch of tissue about the size of a postage stamp. When a sensation hits a receptor it sends an electrical impulse to the brain that converts it into a signal that we can distinguish as a certain scent. Your nose is also close to your mouth and wind pipe so that it can take in air.

The Mouth

Your mouth is located in the front of your head—in a perfect location to take in food—and to project sounds or words to others in communication. Through the mouth the human body takes in both oxygen and food. Its parts include the upper and lower jaws. The upper jaw is stationary, affixed to the skull, while the lower jaw moves up and down as well as side to side to allow chewing. Also in the mouth are teeth and gums, the tongue, and salivary glands that secrete saliva to help break down food—and keep the inside of the mouth moist.

The Ears

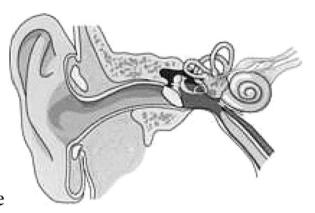

Our two ears are located on either side of our head—so we can determine the direction sound comes from quite well—and the locations help us with orientation and balance. The ear is intricately sculpted with both a shapely outer earlobe and an inner structure that actually welcomes sounds. The ear can hear sounds in the medium range (20-20,000 vibrations or hertz per second) and consists of an auditory canal, semicircular canals, and the eardrum, as well as the intricacies of the hammer, anvil, stirrup, and cochlea, eustachian tubes and tiny hairs called cilia that begin to vibrate when they detect sounds. The vibrations are then conducted to the auditory nerve that sends the signals to the brain.

The Fantastic Human Brain

A scientist recently stated, *"The human brain is the most complex arrangement of matter in the universe."* With 12 billion cells; 120 trillion brain connections, such "strength in numbers" provides the raw materials for the amazing use of your brain. We use a significant part of our brain to read words, hear sounds, and express thoughts—in addition to the controlling of the basic processes of our body. So many things are controlled and impacted by your brain—thought, emotions, social bonding, consciousness, vision and motor skills.

Vision helps contribute to our motor skills. In the process of learning a new activity, such as dancing or riding a bike, the time suddenly comes when it no longer takes as much concentration, because specialized neurons in the cerebellum begin firing in sequence—and so you have LEARNED the action.

This applies to so many of our common activities including baseball.

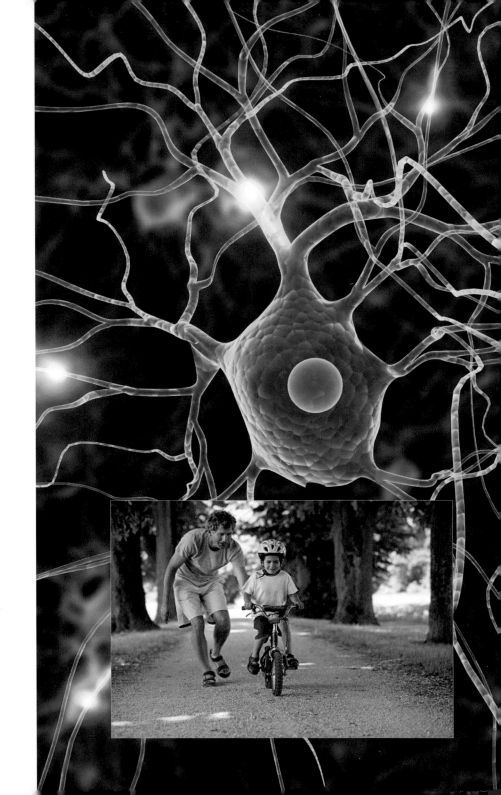

You're up at the Plate, With Bat in Hand!

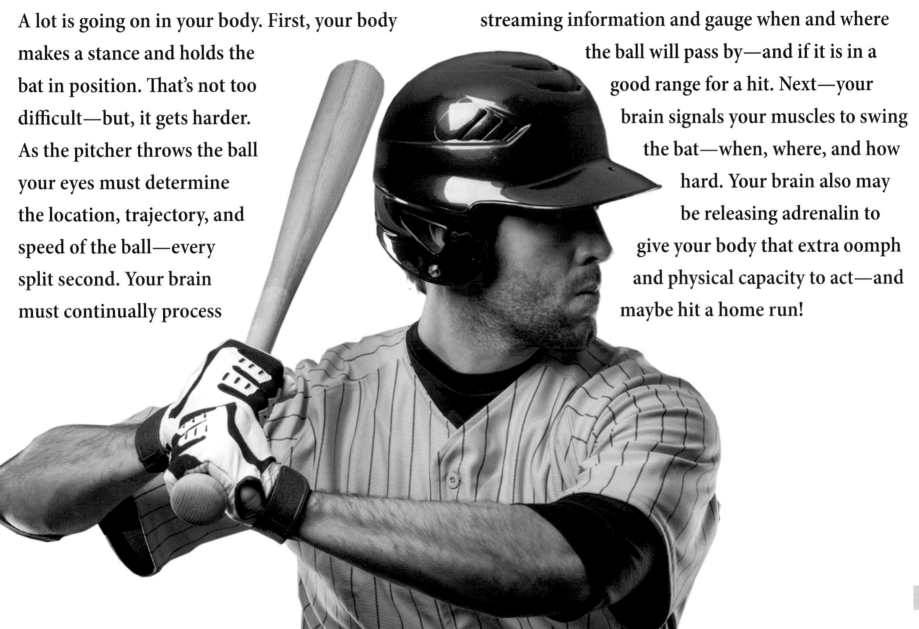

A lot is going on in your body. First, your body makes a stance and holds the bat in position. That's not too difficult—but, it gets harder. As the pitcher throws the ball your eyes must determine the location, trajectory, and speed of the ball—every split second. Your brain must continually process streaming information and gauge when and where the ball will pass by—and if it is in a good range for a hit. Next—your brain signals your muscles to swing the bat—when, where, and how hard. Your brain also may be releasing adrenalin to give your body that extra oomph and physical capacity to act—and maybe hit a home run!

Your Brain's Built-In Emergency Mode

Your body's remarkable ability to respond to danger could scarcely be an act of nature. This has been called the "fight or flight" mechanism of the brain. With danger, your pituitary gland is instructed to secrete adrenaline hormones—then pulse increases, muscles tense, blood pressure increases, eyes dilate, facial muscles tense, perspiration increases, breathing quickens, and more chemicals are secreted to speed blood clotting. *Such changes prepare you for whatever your brain tells you to do next—fight or take flight!*

Each of us May be Gifted

Yes, your Creator has blessed you with a wonderful body—and mind (brain). All of us have inherited something hopefully good from our parents (DNA in action). Instincts and programmed behavior have benefitted us in so many ways!

Then there is "muscle memory" and "practice to make perfect" that comes to our aid.

So, don't look down on education, learning, and practice to help you get "smarter". God has given you gifts and capabilities. He meant for each of us to use them—for our enjoyment and betterment—and to help others—other humans, animals, and our planet!

Thus the heavens and the earth were completed in all their vast array. By the seventh day God had finished the work he had been doing; so on the seventh day he rested from all his work. And God blessed the seventh day and made it holy, because on it he rested from all the work of creating that he had done.

GENESIS 2:1-3

CHAPTER 7

The Seventh Day

It should not surprise us to know that, of all the species on earth, man is the only one with whom He shared information about the creative process. And, the Bible makes clear that our Designer wants us to recognize the need to refresh ourselves and think of Him—at least once a week.

The Fourth Commandment

Remember the Sabbath day by keeping it holy. Six days you shall labor and do all your work, but the seventh day is a Sabbath to the Lord your God.

EXODUS 20:8-10

Many are the plans in a man's heart, but it is the Lord's purpose that prevails.

PROVERBS 19:21

And we know that in all things God works for the good of those who love him, who have been called according to his purpose.

ROMANS 8:28

Therefore, my dear friends, as you have always obeyed—not only in my presence, but now much more in my absence—continue to work out your salvation with fear and trembling, for it is God who works in you to will and to act according to his good purpose.

PHILIPPIANS 2:12-13

In Closing—Solomon Had Some Words for Us

—then I saw all that God has done. No one can comprehend what goes on under the sun. Despite all his efforts to search it out, man cannot discover its meaning. Even if a wise man claims he knows, he cannot really comprehend it.

ECCLESIASTES 8:17

Now all has been heard; here is the conclusion of the matter: fear God and keep his commandments, for this is the whole duty of man. For God will bring every deed into judgment, including every hidden thing, whether it is good or evil.

ECCLESIASTES 12:13-14

About the Author

Jay Schabacker's varied careers—from aerospace to finance to church ministries and theology have led him to recently research and pen the uplifting book—*Purposeful Design*.

A Cornell University education led to accomplishments on aerospace projects including work on the Apollo Moon Program at NASA's Houston Manned Space Center. Later, a Masters of Business Administration (MBA) from the George Washington University prompted him to research and write investment newsletters and start the firm—Schabacker Investment Management. Jay, with the help of Marjory Ross, authored the investment and personal finance book—*Jay Schabacker's Winning in Mutual Funds*, published in 1994 by the American Management Association.

For four decades, Jay has been an enthusiastic benefactor and contributor to numerous Christian organizations and activities. A short list includes: Sunday School Superintendent (Darnestown Presbyterian, Darnestown, MD), Chairman of Board of Trustees (Central Baptist Church, Gaithersburg, MD), Board of Directors (Middle Creek Bible Conference, Gettysburg, PA), Board of Visitors (Southeast Baptist Theological Seminary, Wake Forest, NC), Chairman of the Board (Romanian Christian Enterprises, Washington, DC), and Chairman of the 1992 *Back to Genesis* Washington, D.C. Seminar sponsored by the Institute for Creation Research.

Now an enthusiastic devotee of Bible studies and things eternal, Jay travels with his wife, Nancy, to contemplate the Pyramids of Egypt and the Great Wall of China—studying the marvels of the world around us. The book, *Purposeful Design, Understanding the Creation* about the wonderful world we are honored to live and work in—"the Universe all the way down to the smallest strand of DNA"—is the result of his latest research.

Jay is proud of his four daughters, six grandchildren, and two great-grandchildren. He and his wife, Nancy, now enjoy living on the shore of picturesque Lake Murray in Lexington, South Carolina, where he raises orchids. They are members of the Lexington Presbyterian Church (PCA) of Lexington, South Carolina.

Epilogue—Who Made the Cookies?

"Purposeful Design" may be a new phrase to you.

The words, "Intelligent Design" may be more familiar. The phrase, "Intelligent Design" was coined in the year 1993. At that time, a group of five scientists and professors met on the California coast to discuss the possibility that material and living things might have been painstakingly planned and brought about, not by accident, but by design.

But, this author, feels "Intelligent Design" doesn't go far enough to explain or describe the awesome benevolent "touch" worked by what he calls the "Purposeful Designer"—our Maker—God.

Yes, there is the scientific—and even the "miraculous", but the author would like to invoke the "personal", "human touch" to the creation account for you.

It was done for you and me—lovingly and personally!

As the simplest of examples, take the recipe for making cookies and the results. Intelligence was needed. A recipe, with ingredients, and forethought—but also—the "human touch" —yes,—that of the "maker"!

The author would like you to envision a plate of freshly baked cookies—lovingly created—steaming hot—just starting to cool—on the kitchen counter. And, you cry out, "Who made the cookies?"

Not an abstract accident or occurrence, but someone who loved you very much made them specifically for you—because he or she knew you would love them.

That is the meaning of God's "Purposeful Design"—just for you and me.

In this book, the author wants to share his findings so that you can marvel at (and be thankful for) the love showered on us by a very personal and compassionate God.

Great is the Lord, and most worthy of praise!

PSALM 48:1

Bibliography and Recommended Reading

Barker, Kenneth, General Editor, *The NIV Study Bible—New International Version*, 1985, Zondervan Bible Publishers, Grand Rapids, MI

Batten, Don, *The Revised and Expanded Answers Book,* Thirty-first printing, 2004, Master Books, Inc., P.O. Box 726, Green Forest, AR 72638

Behe, Michael J., *Darwin's Black Box,* 2006, Free Press, a Division of Simon & Shuster, Inc., New York, NY

Brown, Walt, *In the Beginning—Compelling Evidence for Creation and the Flood,* Center for Scientific Creation, www.creationscience.com

Brush, Stephen G., *A History of Modern Planetary Physics, Vol. 3,* 1996, Cambridge University Press, Cambridge, UK

Darwin, Charles, *Origin of Species,* 6th edition, 1988, New York University Press, New York, NY

Davidheiser, Bolton, *Evolution and Christian Faith,* The Presbyterian and Reformed Publishing Company, Third Printing, 1971

Dawkins, Richard, *Climbing Mount Improbable,* 1996, W.W. Norton & Co., New York, NY

Denton, Michael, *Evolution a Theory in Crisis,* 1986, Adler & Adler Publishers

DeYoung, Dr. Donald B., *Astronomy and the Bible—Questions and Answers,* 2nd edition, Baker Books

Epp, Theodore, *The God of Creation,* 1974, Back to the Bible Broadcast, Lincoln, Nebraska

Family World Atlas, 1994, Rand McNally & Co.

Ferrell, Vance, *Evolution Handbook,* 2001, Evolution Facts, Inc., Box 300, Altamont, TN

Ham, Ken, *New Answers Book 1,* Tenth Printing, 2009, Master Books, P.O. Box 726, Green Forest, AR

Ham, Ken, *New Answers Book 2,* Third Printing, 2009, Master Books, P.O. Box 726, Green Forest, AR

Ham, Ken and Taylor, Paul, *The Genesis Solution,* Fifth Printing, 1991, Baker Book House, Grand rapids, MI

Hawkins, Gerald S., *Stonehenge Decoded,* 1965, Doubleday & Company, Inc., Garden City, NY

Hawkins, Stephen W., *A Brief History of Time,* 1988, Bantam Books, New York, NY

Hedtke, Randall, *How the Confirming Evolution Curriculum Violates the First Amendment,* 2007, ACW Press, Nashville, TN

Keller, Timothy, *The Prodigal God,* 2008, Dutton, New York, NY

Kenyon, Dean and Steinman, G., *Biochemical Predestinations,* 1969, McGraw-Hill, New York, NY

LaHaye, Tim, *The Battle for the Mind,* 1980, Fleming H. Revell Company, Old Tappan, NJ

MacArthur, John, *Battle for the Beginning,* 2001, W. Publishing Group, A Division of Thomas Nelson, Inc., Nashville, TN

MacDonald, William, *Believer's Bible Commentary,* 1995, Thomas Nelson Publishers, Nashville, TN

McGee, J. Vernon, *Genesis Chapters 1-15,* 1991, Thomas Nelson, Inc., Nashville, TN

Morris, Henry M., *Biblical Cosmology and Modern Science,* 1970, Craig Press, Nutley, NJ

Morris, Henry M., *Creation: Acts, Fact, and Impacts,* 1974, Creation Life Publishers

Morris, Henry M., *The Genesis Record,* second printing, 1991, Baker Book House, Grand Rapids, MI

Morris, Henry M., *Studies in the Bible and Science,* fourth printing, 1969, Presbyterian and Reformed Publishing Company, Philadelphia, PA

Morris, Henry M. and Others, *A Symposium on Creation,* Master Books, P.O. Box 726, Green Forest, AR

1968, Baker Book House, Grand Rapids, MI

Nelson, Byron C., *After Its Kind,* nineteenth printing, 1970, Bethany Fellowship, Inc., Minneapolis, MN

Patten, Donald W., *The Biblical Flood and the Ice Epoch,* 1966, Pacific Meridian Publishing Co., Seattle, WA

Patten, Donald W., *A Symposium on Creation II,* 1971, Baker Book House, Grand Rapids, MI

Patten, Donald W., *A Symposium on Creation III,* 1971, Baker Book House, Grand Rapids, MI

Patten, Donald W., Hatch, Ronald R., Steinhauer, Loren C., *The Long Day of Joshua and Six Other Catastrophes,* 1973, Pacific Meridian Publishing Co., Seattle, WA

Powell, Doug, *Guide to Christian Apologetics,* 2006, Holman Reference, Nashville, TN

Shute, Evan, *Flaws in the Theory of Evolution,* fourth printing, 1969, Craig Press, Nutley, NY

Strobel, Lee, *The Case for the Creator,* 2004, Zondervan, Grand Rapids, MI

Strong, James, *Strong's Exhaustive Concordance of the Bible,* McDonald Publishing Co., McLean, VA

Whitcomb, John C., Morris, Henry M., *The Genesis Flood,* 1961, Baker Book House, Grand Rapids, MI

Wiker, Benjamin, Witt, Jonathan, *A Meaningful World,* 2006, Inter Varsity Press

Wolfson, Glen W., *The 1993 Midwest Floods and Rapid Canyon Formation,* Sept. 1994, Creative Research Society Quarterly

Wysong, R.L., *The Creation – Evolution Controversy,* eighth printing, 1976, Inquiry Press, Midland, MI

Yancey, Philip D., *Prayer: Does It Make Any Difference?,* 2006, Zondervan, Grand Rapids, MI

Young, Davis A.., *Christianity & The Age of the Earth,* 1982, Zondervan, Grand Rapids, MI

Purposeful Design *Young Explorer's Club*

Workbook Curriculum

Dear Mom or Dad,

Now is the perfect time to ***"join the club"!***

Yes, now that you have your copy of the evangelical book, ***Purposeful Design – Understanding the Creation***, we all can explore the amazing wonders that our Lord God has done for us - and our children.

Speaking of our children, I devised the ***Young Explorer's Club*** for your children - to increase their experience, understanding, and comprehension as they *explore* the book's chapters – Day One thru Day Seven.

The workbooks are short, sweet, and fun. Each chapter set contains a Kid's Workbook (with questions), a Teacher's Set (with answers), and a Certificate of Completion.

As children of various ages and grades have varying levels of comprehension, moms/dads (the teachers) will readily see ways to adjust their approach to maximize the child's learning. Please help with answers where needed. As we collect your feedback and experiences, we plan to expand to three or more different sets of Workbooks (such as preschool, elementary, and high school).

Please go to our website www.Jayschabacker.com, or to www.Purposefuldesign.net

and download the kid's workbook "Free Curriculum."

You will note that the workbooks are structured to make the youngsters THINK, stretch their minds and comprehension, and become more aware of some of the Bible's wonderful scriptures - and, even pray! Do you have any suggestions for what you'd like to see us add?

Please get back to me by email at Jayschab@aol.com about your "young explorer" experience, so that I may move ahead with changes and improvements as needed.

Thanks for joining "the club." In Christ,

Jay Schabacker